Muttering Doggerel

Muttering Doggerel

POEMS FROM A DOG'S PERSPECTIVE

With help from Liz Cowley

NINE
ELMS
BOOKS

Muttering Doggerel
First published in 2023 by
Nine Elms Books
Unit 1g, Clapham North Arts Centre
26–32 Voltaire Road
London SW4 6DH

Email: info@nineelmsbooks.co.uk
www.nineelmsbooks.co.uk

ISBN: 978-1-910533-71-0
eBook: 978-1-910533-72-7

Cover design, typesetting and illustrations: Tony
Hannaford.
Printed in India.

IMPOSSIBLE!

'No dogs can dream up poetry!'
We know you'd say that straight away.
But why not turn a page or two?
With luck, you'll change your mind today!

Of course we needed human help.
We can't use pens - that's sadly true.
But planting verse in someone's head
is something that we've learned to do.

We think it's called 'telepathy' –
transferring thoughts, but silently –
and poetry, we're glad to say,
and goodness me, how luckily!

Thankfully, we know Liz Cowley.
She listened – and so patiently
and wrote our poem down for us.
A dream became reality!

You own a dog? You'll like this book.
At least,we hope that may be true.
But if you don't, we'll never cry.
You'll know that's something dogs can't do!

HOUSE RULES

So many things we dogs can't do.
The list would make you furious!
We understand them – most of them,
but others make us curious.

We're not allowed to tug our leads,
and mostly banished from your bed.
We're not allowed to bark at you,
or scoff at any food we're fed.

We're not allowed to hog the fire,
or bare our teeth – my goodness, no!
And not supposed to show we're cross,
or rest on laps like years ago.

We're not allowed to jump on you,
and not allowed to moan or whine.
These days, I often ask myself
why *are* my owners friends of mine?

We're not allowed out, not at night,
and not allowed out on our own
(only outside in the garden),
and not allowed to groan and moan.

Gosh, would you like to be a dog
with all the rules we tolerate?
There's always yet another one..
we never have that long to wait!

A SOFA

Are *you* allowed to lie on one?
Yes? Lucky you! I'm firmly not,
in case I cover it with hairs
which tend to drop off quite a lot.

The size I am – that ought to help.
I hardly take up any space,
but have to sit down on the floor
or find myself another place.

Dogs all love to lie on sofas
(and when you're out, we sometimes do).
But when we hear you coming back,
we jump off them – and quickly too!

Luckily, we have good hearing,
and know just when you're at the door –
and leap off sofas instantly
and sit politely, on the floor!

We even tuck the cushions back
and re-arrange them in a row.
We dogs are mostly clever things,
much brighter than you'll ever know!

MOVING HOUSE

Oh dear, you're moving house again!
What's wrong with it – the one you've got?
I'm scared you'll leave my toys behind.
Last time you moved, I lost the lot!

It's misery to watch you pack
and tossing things into a bin,
while never guessing that I'm scared
and happy with the house we're in.

No pets like moving, none of us,
and going off to somewhere new.
Upheaval – horrible for us,
and always rather frightening too!

Just when we pets get used to things
you move on to another place.
It makes me want to learn to cry
and show the tears upon my face.

And will there be a garden there,
and pleasant places for a walk?
Not shedding tears is tough enough.
It's even worse we dogs can't talk.

Pets are worth consideration
when moving to another place.
You think we'll be content with that?
Last thing we'll wear – a happy face!

BACK FROM A PARTY

My mistress said she'd 'had a ball.'
But where's she put it? *I* don't know.
I'd love to have another ball –
a new one that she'd like to throw!

Perhaps she left the ball behind,
or maybe it's still in the car.
If it is, I wish she'd fetch it.
Impatient? Doggies often are!

But 'balls', I think, mean different things,
and shouting '*BALLS!*' is horrible.
Perhaps it's not a gift for me –
or one I might find miserable!

Balls should all be pleasant presents,
but maybe they are sometimes not.
I guess I should be quite content
to stick with it – the one I've got!

I've bitten it so many times,
it's not the ball it used to be.
But stay puffed up, it always does.
It's more than earned my loyalty!

NOT A DOG'S DELIGHT!

My gosh, the postman drives me mad!
He drops in letters every day
which always makes me barking mad.
I wish the chap would stay away!

I always bark – I can't help that
when someone stuffs things through the door –
but very often ask myself
'Whatever am I barking for?'

I guess the noise just worries me.
My ears prick up in seconds flat.
I'll never like the sound of it –
when letters plop upon the mat!

Disturbing? Yes, for me it is for me,
and not that nice for owners too –
that's if they turn out to be bills.
They're never any fun for you!

All sudden sounds – horrible,
and things we never want to hear.
All dogs are quite afraid of them,
and things we quickly learn to fear!

THE FRONT DOOR

Dammit! Please don't ever slam it
when dogs just want to say 'Goodbye'!
We're nice enough to see you off –
so slam it in our faces? Why?

Just close it softly – that's more kind,
and surely, better manners too.
What's more, a parting stroke is nice.
Is that too much to ask of you?

They're sad enough – the hours ahead –
that's if you'll be away all day.
So when we come to see you off,
don't slam the door, then rush away!

So many people owning dogs
just never think of things like that.
It's something that you ought to do.
Too much to ask – a parting pat?

A TOUGH LIFE

Do humans *ever, ever* guess
just how frustrating life can be –
that's if we're pups, and still so young
we can't learn words that easily?

'Off!' – that's the first word that we know,
and 'Down!' – that's soon the second one,
and 'Out!' – that's usually the third,
All words we pets don't find much fun.

'Here!' – that's a word we far prefer.
It means you want our company.
And what's more, if you pat your lap –
that's heavenly for pups like me!

UPSTAIRS

I wonder what it's like upstairs?
That's something lots of dogs don't know.
We'd love to climb up and explore,
Why *should* we stay a floor below?

Downstairs – that's fine, it's comfortable,
but then, the older that we grow,
we long to see the things up there,
But ever do that? Firmly no!

Jump over them – the gates they've got?
We can't. Alas, we're not that tall,
and if we tried to jump that high,
we know we'd have a nasty fall!

We live with curiosity –
it's something most pets have to do,
but frequently, frustratedly –
If only all our owners knew!

FEAR

Your cat has always made it clear
she never wants to play with me,
clearly frightened of a doggy –
the *last* thing that she wants to see!

Are *all* cats so afraid of dogs?
If so, then what an awful shame!
I'd love to be a friend of hers,
but no, she doesn't feel the same.

And if I'm sitting by the fire,
she never curls up close to me.
But why? Because she thinks I'll bite?
For me, that's such a tragedy.

We dogs and cats can be great friends,
in spite of all our differences.
So what a shame it often is
that cats see dogs as enemies!

'SIT!'

Gosh, that's a word that makes me cross!
Why *should* I always have to sit
when people come inside the house?
Why can't I sniff them out a bit?

Sitting down can be frustrating,
though humans never seem to mind.
We dogs all like to sniff around.
Not notice that? You must be blind!

You humans never smell the same.
It's interesting to find that out.
And what else are our noses for?
Of course, we need to sniff about!

Our sense of smell serves us so well,
we always sniff out enemies.
It's clearly something *you* can't do,
and what a dreadful shame that is!

And friends or foes? We know at once.
We work that out in seconds flat.
You ought to watch us rather more,
but never seem to think of that.

Terrific critics – dogs all are.
We notice things you never do –
and always sniff out loyal friends -
the ones deserving trust from you!

A FREQUENT NEED

I have to go outside to poo.
I'm not allowed to use your loo,
because I couldn't pull the chain –
I have to go outside again.

And when at last, I'm let outside,
like every dog, I take a pride
in hiding poo away from you –
that's something all dogs ought to do!

What? Use the lawn? Good heavens, no!
That's something dogs all firmly know.
We never need advice from you –
our instinct tells us, quickly too.

No terrier is merrier
than one who's loved as much as me.
But that depends – tremendously
on where I pick to poo or pee!

A lavatory? What luxury!
But no, I'll never sit on one.
Has *any* dog? I doubt that's true.
A thing, perhaps, we've never done!

DOUBLE BEDS

Gosh, why do humans share their beds?
A thing we dogs would *hate* to do.
We need to have a private place,
and not a bed that's made for two!

Another dog here in my bed?
The very thought is misery!
Thank God our owners realize
we dogs prefer our privacy.

You've got two dogs? Then buy two beds!
To make us share one? Misery!
We rarely want to cuddle up
as humans do quite happily!

Dogs aren't groaners (like some owners),
but moan we would – and instantly,
if ever forced to share a bed
as humans do, contentedly.

LATE NIGHT TELLY

When humans find they're getting bored,
you soon 'switch off' as dogs all do.
But if you're bored and go to bed,
please *do* switch off the telly too!

We can't do that, although we've tried.
It's just not what a paw is for.
We try and reach the bits to press,
then topple backwards on the floor!

Watching telly – sometimes pleasant,
but reaching knobs is never fun.
So please don't leave that up to pets.
Among the worst things that you've done!

I need to stick this poem up,
and right in front of their TV.
With any luck, they'll get the hint.
A huge relief for pets like me!

I like to hear the latest news,
exactly as all humans do.
But *please* don't leave the telly on.
Is that too much to ask of you?

WATCHING YOU KNITTING

Sitting knitting, needles clicking –
a pleasant thing to hear and see.
But *please* don't knit dogs anything.
One coat's enough - not two or three!

A woolly jumper? Most unwelcome!
In Summer, the *last* thing we need.
They'd make us far too hot at once -
and more so, if a fluffy breed!

In Winter? Maybe bearable,
but not a thing we'd like to wear.
My goodness, how embarrassing
if other doggies stop and stare!

We know you'd make us pretty things.
But wear them? No, what misery!
It's nice to see you sit and knit –
but please, no clothes for dogs like me!

Clicking, knitting – that's a nice thing,
We listen to that, happily.
Most dogs enjoy the sound of it,
but worried, we can sometimes be!

YOU CHILDREN

You children are at school again.
We pets all miss your company.
Why *do* you go there quite so much?
That often saddens dogs like me.

You clearly have a lot to learn,
but learn one thing – you never do.
And what is that? We dogs get sad
without the sight and sound of you.

And if our owners go to work,
that adds to it, our misery.
Why *can't* you learn to work at home?
To me, that's such a mystery!

We try and find new things to do,
but what, without your company?
Perhaps you shouldn't own a pet,
or one as sociable as me!

SLEEPING

I sleep downstairs, as most dogs do,
and do that more than happily.
At times, we need to be alone
and treasure hours of privacy.

You potter off, and up to bed
and make quite sure I've gone to mine.
With luck, I'll get a final pat.
If not, a stupid time to whine!

You humans seem to talk so much,
we need a restful place to be,
not listening to you late at night –
and surely, understandably!

Dreamland – lovely place for doggies!
A place we're always *off* the lead
and free to roam contentedly.
To hear you chat – *last* thing we need!

'DOWN!'

'Down!' is not a word I like.
In fact, a word that all dogs hate.
We like to put our paws on you.
Why *do* you get in such a state?

Why *should* we stay down all the time?
It's boring sitting on the floor,
and never jumping up to greet
a visitor who's at the door.

And what if dogs barked 'DOWN!' at you?
I'm sure you'd all be very cross.
So why do that when friends arrive?
It leaves us at a total loss!

Perhaps you think we'll topple them
and make them fall down on the floor.
I guess there *is* a risk of that,
but staying down is such a bore!

DOGS AND DAILIES

Your daily – not a friend of mine.
She always tidies things away –
and where they might be hard to find.
Thank God she's not here every day!

And hoovering? A nasty noise –
and one that dogs me in a trice,
and when she does that, all round me,
and moves my bed – that *isn't* nice.

And worse, she shakes my bedding out,
just when it's nice and snug for me,
so when it's time to go to bed,
I don't sleep quite as comfortably.

Luckily, she's just a 'weekly'
and not a daily misery.
Why she's ever called a 'daily'
is yet another mystery.

No dogs and dailies make great pals,
and dogs should not be blamed for that.
Adore us? No, they just ignore us
and rarely give us pets a pat.

They always think we're in the way,
and stopping all the jobs get done,
unless they banish us outside.
And when it's raining – not much fun!

TICKLING BACKS

Tickling backs – so irritating!
I have to wriggle on the floor.
I wish my owners guessed at once
just why I'm wriggling, and what for.

Thank God they've got a scratchy mat,
but that's outside the kitchen door.
If only they would open it.
I can't stand tickles any more!

Most other dogs are luckier.
You get less tickles, with less fur.
But if you had a coat like mine,
a smoother one you'd far prefer!

A RAILWAY ROOM

My master owns a railway room
and wanders round it every day
to play with all his model trains.
It often takes my breath away!

Do other humans have such rooms?
I've never seen one, if they do.
Perhaps there isn't room for one.
I'm not surprised if that is true.

But what an age it took to make!
It meant a lot less walks for me.
But did I mind? Well, now and then,
but chose to hide that speedily!

What other dogs have things to see
that quickly take their breath away?
None! Or not one that I've met.
The sight of it just makes my day!

BATTERSEA DOGS HOME

Alas, I'm living in a home
for all unwanted dogs like me,
hoping someone nice will buy me.
All I can do is wait and see.

I'm not alone, a load of dogs
are living here in Battersea,
all hoping that we'll find a home
and with a kindly family.

Perhaps you'd like to buy a dog –
and hopefully, a dog like me.
If so, please arrange a visit.
I need a new home, urgently.

The carers here are wonderful,
but still, I need a family –
and not a life with lots of dogs,
despite their pleasant company.

You'd like to buy a spaniel pup?
If so, please come to Battersea.
I'd love to be a family pet,
and surely, understandably!

TONGUES

You've dropped a soup bowl on the floor
but please don't go and fetch a mop!
We dogs will lick it up for you.
We love to see the mess you drop!

Our tongues are always willing things,
and ones you rarely seem to use.
But dogs like me all love our tongues –
the things that we'd most hate to lose!

If food is always just the same
of course our meals become a bore.
We'd love to taste some different things -
a nice surprise we'd all adore!

'Variety – the spice of life'
That's something that you often say.
What's more we pets agree with you,
so why feed us the same each day?

We're well-fed, yes – but fed up too,
with never a surprise in store.
But none of us much wants to starve.
Although our meals are such a bore!

BIRTHDAY PARTIES

Wow, how nice to have a party
with other friendly dogs we know!
But will we ever see that day?
We gave up hope, and years ago.

Yes, I've been to human parties,
and seen you eat a lovely cake.
But do I ever get a slice?
Please give me one, for heavens's sake!

You greedy little girls and boys!
What? Never, ever, think of me?
You *must* have noticed that I drool,
though always disappointedly.

I guess to drool is far from cool –
a terrible mistake to make –
dreadful manners at a party.
Small wonder we're not given cake!

Just half a slice would be so nice,
though even that's a rarity.
All parties (if we go to them)
are times to hide our jealousy!

A DOG'S DINNER

How very odd that's what you say –
that's if you don't like what you see
when someone's made a mess of things.
But what's it got to do with me?

Dogs' dinners are a lovely sight.
I know all dogs would quite agree.
How curious to use those words.
To me, a total mystery.

Dinner stops us getting thinner.
We need to eat, like humans do.
What's more, most dogs are pretty slim.
We rarely put on weight like you!

CHOCOLATES

All chocolates – dangerous for dogs,
or so our owners always say.
And if that's true, how sad that is,
especially on Christmas Day.

We know it isn't cool to drool.
That's something we try *not* to do.
But why are they so dangerous?
Is that a lie, or is it true?

They never do *you* any harm,
so why should chocolates make us ill?
If only you would tell us why
but know you never ever will.

And if you're right, don't eat such things –
well, not in front of dogs like me.
That isn't very kind of you.
And drool to see that? Yes, we will!

Just *one* choc would be heavenly,
before you tuck the box away.
But try and find it? No, we don't!
A tick-off would quite spoil the day!

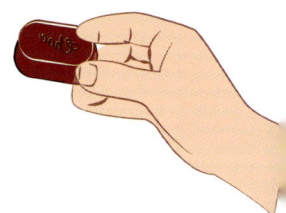

FOOD

Of course you all like eating out,
but feed us please, before you go.
That's if you won't be back for hours –
a thing all owners ought to know!

And fetch a tin and open it?
That's something that our paws can't do.
Instead, we have to sit and drool
while feeling furious with you!

And as for going out so late
and then returning – straight to bed –
for dogs, that's such a misery,
especially when we've not been fed!

GOSH!

My gosh, what's that upon your plate?
It looks to me as if it's meat.
But whose? I hope it's not from dogs!
To watch you eat is *not* a treat!

Better not to think about it,
exactly as I've learned to do.
And if you humans love us dogs,
I tell myself that *can't* be true!

And after all, we dogs eat meat,
and so, it seems, does every cat.
Certain questions – best unanswered.
We need to learn to live with that!

A HOT DOG

Today my owners ate a 'hot dog' –
I hope not made from dogs like me.
I couldn't bear to watch them eat!
I ran away – and instantly!

'*Here*, have a 'hot dog!' – scary words!
I shivered, and from head to toe.
It's better that I don't find out.
It's something I don't want to know!

What, kill a dog and eat it up?
My gosh, I hope that isn't true.
I wouldn't like my owners much
if that's a thing they want to do!

They *surely* couldn't eat a dog!
The very thought is agony.
But when I study human life,
then nothing much surprises me.

A DOGGIE MOAN

My food is always in a bowl,
and never on a plate like yours.
I guess you think I'd make a mess,
and muck up what you call your 'floors'.

I'd love to see a pretty plate.
How very pleasant that would be!
But no. I'm stuck with plastic bowls.
No plates are put in front of me!

I guess it's hard to understand
what all we dogs would far prefer.
The only thing you know at once?
How much we like strokes on our fur!

Oh yes, and walks – you're good at that.
A thing we all appreciate.
That's if we get enough of them
and don't have several days to wait!

EASTER

Now, what on earth is Eastertime?
A time you don't like dogs about!
Well, not with all those lovely eggs –
You hate it – when our tongues hang out.

And why buy eggs? Especially now,
and wrap them up so prettily?
Yes, you're clearly celebrating,
But what? We can't guess easily.

'Feastertime' – a better name
With all those lovely eggs to eat.
A day all dogs look forward to,
while hoping for a change from meat!

You mention Jesus. That can please us.
A chap to solve the mystery?
But what's he got to do with eggs?
Another thing that baffles me!

Gosh, did he ever lay an egg?
And what is more, a chocolate one?
Well, if he did, how nice of him!
He clearly had a sense of fun.

But eat a lovely easter egg?
That's something so few dogs can do.
Well, as we've heard, chocs make us ill.
My goodness me, we envy you!

A HAPPY PUPPY

Lucky me - you've left a biscuit!
Eat it? Maybe. Should I risk it?
Why not? We pups deserve a treat,
and biscuits make a change from meat.

Delicious! I've just eaten it.
Too tempting left upon a plate.
I couldn't simply look at it.
And goodness me, the taste was great!

Why *shouldn't* puppies taste nice things,
exactly as our owners do?
You're lucky you can choose your food,
At times, I really envy you!

PLATES

We dogs all learn to lick a plate.
Why *is* it something *you* don't do?
You always put them in the sink.
But why? We'd clean them up for you.

We'd lick them clean, and instantly.
Why wash them up? Mad thing to do!
A waste of water, and of time.
We wish that's something that you knew!

We dogs can clean up splendidly,
much faster than dishwashers do.
Just put the plates upon the floor.
For all us pets, a dream come true!

MY OWNERS

Both of them are on a 'diet'.
They seem to think they've grown too fat.
What *does* it matter, getting fatter?
And why can't they just live with that?

Doggies all adore our dinners,
and never seem to put on weight.
These days it's rather sad to see
a smaller portion on your plate!

For us, one tin can keep us thin,
and thinner than we ought to be.
But ask you for a bit more food?
Dogs can't do that, not easily!

FAT HOPE

My owners eat three meals a day,
but one is all I ever get.
Perhaps they think I'd get too fat –
and wouldn't want a fatter pet.

Luckily, I'm rarely hungry
as humans often seem to be.
Perhaps one meal is quite enough
to keep me living healthily.

Goodness – breakfast, lunch and dinner
would be a lot too much for me,
and maybe why you're 'dieting' –
and frankly not surprisingly!

I shouldn't think of things like that.
It's something pets should never do,
but simply can't help noticing
we rarely get as fat as you!

PHONES AND GROANS!

A dog – a friend you *shouldn't* own,
that's if in love – and with your phone!
My goodness me, you talk and talk
when dogs are waiting for a walk!

And when, *at last*, you've said goodbye,
the rain starts pelting from the sky.
Your phones – a dreadful enemy.
They shorten walks too frequently.

What *do* you get to talk about
just when we need a nice trip out?
And why not ever learn to talk
and *after* we've all had a walk!

Of course your phone can make us groan,
and make us grizzly instantly.
But maybe things you ought to own,
in case there's an emergency.

'LOCKDOWN'

Now, that's a word you humans hate!
You loathe to live less sociably.
It's clearly why you've bought more dogs
to make up for lost company.

We've heard that sales of dogs have soared.
We poodle crosses, cockapoos
all think the lockdown's wonderful –
for all of us, it's splendid news!

Terrific for all walkers too –
they're in demand – and more and more.
They used to walk a single dog,
but now they walk with three or four!

And cyclists? Most are learning fast
to swerve away from dogs like me.
Owning dogs? That's more than trebled.
That's why you ride more cautiously!

'BALLS!'

That's something that my owners say,
and often do, that's if they're cross.
All dogs think balls are wonderful –
a thing we love to see you toss!

My balls – among my favourite toys.
It's always such fun fetching one.
That quickly makes me wag my tail –
among the nicest things I've done!

So why shout 'BALLS!' so angrily?
That simply makes no sense to me.
I guess I'll never ever know.
Oh dear, another mystery!

It clearly means you're getting cross,
and don't agree with what you've heard.
But balls, for pets, are such nice things,
we'd far prefer another word!

A WINTER WONDER

Today, when taken to the park,
I saw a man made out of snow,
and watched you children making balls,
and clearly ones you liked to throw.

Of course I ran straight after them,
and quickly too, although I'm old,
but spat them out and straight away.
My goodness, they were icy cold!

Throwing snowballs at each other?
For dogs, the oddest thing to do.
The only balls I'll ever like
are warm ones I retrieve for you!

You ought to know some dogs fear snow,
and find our walks a wee bit tough,
as if it's freezing cold out there,
our coats may not be warm enough!

At times, you just don't understand
we fear the cold – that's if we're old.
But still, we'll go out – cautiously.
We need to stay 'as good as gold'.

Signs that we are getting older
aren't welcome – all dogs know that's true.
Owners never want to see them,
unless they're getting ancient too!

A PAIN IN THE NECK

I wish you wouldn't tug my lead,
or yank it as you sometimes do.
It's not my fault I walk so fast.
I'd hate to be as slow as you.

Why have a dog who walks this fast,
that's if you can't keep up with me?
You should have bought a slower one,
or learn to walk more speedily!

I used to be a happy dog.
That's when I was a little pup.
My walks were far more fun back then.
If only I could speed you up!

But then, I've guessed you're getting old,
so that is most unfair of me.
Of course, you're slowing down a lot.
At least, it's not a mystery.

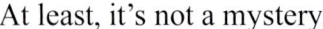

A HEATWAVE

When the weather's getting colder,
of course, you need a coat like me.
But I don't need another one.
In Winter, I'm dressed perfectly.

It's Summertime that gets me down.
My coat can make me far too hot,
and cross that I can't take it off.
My favourite months? No, firmly not!

I wonder if you've thought of that?
I don't think many humans do,
or notice that we seek out shade
because we need it more than you.

The kindest thing your parents do?
Live in a place that's got a tree –
a space to lie and in the shade.
That's heavenly for dogs like me!

Or else, please use the garden hose,
and turn it on – and frequently,
not just to water all the plants,
but cool down all hot dogs like me!

We'd love a spray, and every day –
the fastest treat to beat the heat.
A dog who doesn't love your hose?
That's not a pet I'll ever meet!

A COMMON THOUGHT

Now, would she be a dog I'd like,
and one I'd rather like to know?
Owners ought to talk to strangers
who've got another dog in tow.

The chance of new friends – surely nice.
More humans ought to think of that
when meeting strangers on a walk.
So why not pause, and have a chat?

Dogs could get to know each other,
and so could more dog owners too.
I wonder why you're mostly shy
and walk on by, the way you do.

A common thought it is for me,
each time I see another pet.
But talk to strangers on a walk?
A thing I've never seen – not yet!

You smile at them, then walk on by,
and goodness me, how sad is that?
You humans need to understand
we'd love another friendly pat!

NO, I'M NOT A JOLLY DOGGY!

I've just been taken to a vet.
My fault – I bit the neighbour's cat.
But then she bit me twice as hard –
so hard, I couldn't cope with that!

The vet was kind, he patched me up
and wrapped my leg in bandages.
But now I'm terrified of cats
and think they're my worst enemies!

My goodness me, their claws are sharp,
and so, alas, are all their teeth.
The row on top is bad enough
without the other one beneath!

Gosh! Just one bite was such a fright –
enough to send me straight to bed.
And goodness, all the blood I shed.
In fact, it's lucky I'm not dead!

VET BILLS

No pet much likes to see a vet,
and any more than owners do.
We know they'll get a whacking bill –
enough to make them feel ill too!

And if we don't need that much help,
that's something vets will never say.
They love to find things wrong with us –
a quick way to increase their pay!

More inspection? An injection?
They'll quickly think of things to do.
I'd place a bet there's not one vet
who doesn't want more cash from you!

But maybe that's unfair to vets,
and if so, our apologies.
We know you'll never put this book
on tables in your surgeries!

HOW OLD AM I?

How old am I? Well, don't ask me!
It's something that we dogs don't know.
We only know we're getting old
when things become too hard to do.

We find that we can't run as fast,
and sleep for longer, all too true,
and can't jump up inside a car
as quickly as we used to do.

We feel the cold a whole lot more,
as I suspect old people do,
and eat much less, and don't want walks –
not when we can't keep up with you.

We see the vet more frequently,
and start to fear him more and more.
We know that he could 'put us down' –
a thought that shocks us to the core.

Our owners live much longer lives
than any dog can hope to do.
Of course that's something we accept,
although at times, we envy you.

But, oh, the worst thing you can do
is buy a pup before we die!
That tells us that our end is near
and makes us wish that we could cry!

KISSING

How funny watching humans kiss!
That's something that no creature does.
It's something that you seem to love.
It clearly gives you all a buzz!

Our mouths are there to help us eat
and lick things – all they ever do,
And press them on another mouth?
For us, that's *not* a dream come true!

Kissing – something we're not missing,
and never will, I'm sure that's true.
It's quite enough to cuddle us.
That's all we ever need from you!

THE HEIGHT OF BLISS!

Last night I dreamed that I was human,
and had two legs like humans do.
And goodness, what a gorgeous dream!
What fun it was to stand like you!

Walking on 'all fours' is boring,
though other dogs might not agree.
That's if they are bigger, taller –
and not a little chap like me!

What? Scuttling round upon the floor?
That's not a thing we like to do.
We'd love to learn to stand up straight –
and look you in the eye – that, too!

However difficult it seems,
please try and understand our dreams.
Is that too much to ask of you?
We dearly hope that isn't true!

CROSSPATCHES!

You 'lose' your tempers – now and then.
But help you find them? No, pets won't.
They're better lost – and instantly.
And search around? Of course, we don't!

All tempers should be hidden things,
and tucked away in seconds flat.
I don't think there's a single pet
who wouldn't quite agree with that.

Do pets have tempers? Probably,
but things we wouldn't dare to lose.
You wouldn't love us half as much –
the *last* friends that you'd ever choose!

Of course, we dogs get cross at times.
But make that clear? We rarely do.
You'd soon be twice as cross with us,
especially if we barked at you!

Always happy? Never snappy?
Good-tempered, we can't *always* be.
You irritate us now and then,
which shouldn't be a mystery!

TEARS

Burst into tears? Pets never do.
We think it's very strange of you.
How odd it is – the human race –
we'd hate to have tears on our face!

Wet faces? So uncomfortable!
We'd rather keep ours nice and dry.
But you don't seem to mind at all,
that's when you're sad and start to cry!

Wet tears, which make it hard to see?
My goodness what a misery!
And dropping down upon your cheeks?
We'd mop them up more speedily!

Quite clearly you've heard awful news.
Of course, we guess that straight away.
But still, they baffle us – your tears.
And in your eyes, we wish they'd stay!

But all the same, if spotting tears,
most pets would love to comfort you.
But ever try and lick your cheeks?
Your height makes that too hard to do!

NAMES

When thinking of a name for dogs,
A wee bit of advice for you –
Please guess it needs two syllables
(Or three or four) – wise things to do!

When calling for us on a walk,
A name like Jack or John is mad.
You always have to lengthen it,
And when you do, we're more than glad.

Jacky, Johnny, Muffin, Tinker –
All names like that are sensible.
It's something owners ought to know –
one syllable is miserable.

It's such a shame you pick a name
that's far too short for us – and you.
Why is it humans don't guess that?
Well, don't ask me. I wish I knew!

tyberius

PAWS

Your hands – much cleverer than paws.
You pick up things so easily.
We dogs all have to use our teeth,
and do that, but frustratedly.

I bet you never think of paws
and all the things they'll never do,
and why we envy human hands.
Perhaps a big surprise for you!

And as for fingers – lucky you!
So much more useful than our claws.
And as for standing up so straight,
we envy that stuck on all fours!

But then, we promise you they're rare –
our sudden bouts of jealousy.
We learn to live with what we've got,
 and for the most part, happily!

WALKING DOWN THE HIGH STREET

My owners now need walking sticks,
and walk so slowly – sad for me.
I hate the way they yank my lead.
For me, that's such a misery!

I wish they'd trust me *off* the lead.
They clearly don't – I know that's true.
They've told themselves I'd run away –
a thing I wouldn't want to do.

Perhaps I'd run ahead of them,
but then I'd sit and wait a bit.
I wish they knew, I really do.
Fun walks in town? The opposite!

Most golden oldies, golden-hearted,
but need to learn a thing or two –
like trusting us a good deal more –
a thing they often fail to do!

No older doggies need a lead –
it's time you had more faith in us.
But do you? All too often, no,
which sometimes makes us furious!

Desert you? No, we never would.
So why not learn to trust us more?
The *last* thing that we'd ever do
is leave the owners we adore!

A BURGLAR

Today, I'm such a happy dog!
I heard a burglar breaking in,
and bit him! Goodness me, he yelled.
In fact, he made an awful din!

One bite, much better than a fight.
For me, a safer thing to do.
Just one – enough to see him off,
and make a painful exit too!

My owners quickly came downstairs
and watched me chase him to the door.
What heaven, all the strokes I got!
Just one or two? No, many more!

And now I've helped them yet again.
And how? I licked the carpet clean.
He left a drop or two of blood –
how terrified he must have been!

Now, I'm feeling quite a hero.
My owners are so proud of me,
they're giving me a load more strokes.
They know, for me, that's heavenly!

Burglars? No, of course not welcome.
But if we chase one out – what bliss!
Thought a hero? Showered with cuddles?
I wish more days were just like this!

MOANS AND GROANS

Moaners? Groaners? Cross with owners?
That's something we dogs rarely are.
And shake our heads at you? We don't.
We all know that's a step too far!

We need your love, and you need ours.
You make that clear to pets like me.
We cheer you up, and so do you.
That helps us all live happily!

Equal love – our greatest blessing.
And every time you make that plain,
we get to love you more and more
and count our blessings yet again!

But if you're shopping, hurry up!
We hate to wait – stuck in the car.
You surely don't need all that food!
Are you more hungry than we are?

The only time we're driven mad
is when we're waiting – endlessly.
There's one thing we prefer to food –
the pleasure of your company!

PET FRAUD

We dogs have heard we're often bought
because we're sold as 'pedigrees'.
A lie? You need to check that out,
as money doesn't grow on trees!

Some humans pay a bomb for dogs
you're sold, when told we're all pure bred –
and then find out we're clearly not
which keeps you wide awake in bed.

Before you buy us, take a test
to see if we're pure pedigrees –
a thing you always ought to do
before you fork out legal fees!

But then you might adore your pets,
although we're more than ordinary.
We don't need to be pedigrees
to keep you living happily!

100% GENUINE MUTT

A SAD DAY FOR DOGS

You humans never sell your kids,
but sell ours? Yes, you often do.
You've never guessed we get depressed.
You simply can't believe that's true.

We wish you did. To lose them all
is always such a misery.
You *really* think that dogs don't mind?
We often do – a tragedy!

Use our kids to make you money?
That's not a pleasant thing to do.
Humans mostly love their children,
and pets are just the same as you.

We always mourn to see them go,
and often wonder where they've gone,
and why we never visit them.
It's sometimes hard to carry on.

You can't afford to feed them all?
Then, please don't ever make us mate.
What? Never get to know our kids?
Of course, that's something that we hate.

BREEDING

What? Breed from me? Please don't do that.
A thing I hope you never do.
What? Forced to mate with other pets,
and even worse, in front of you?

And what's the point of having babes
I'll never, ever, get to know?
And watch me mating? Ghastly thought.
I'd hate my private parts on show!

Hoping that you'll see me mating
is something that you shouldn't do.
And what if I'm not in the mood
and end up disappointing you?

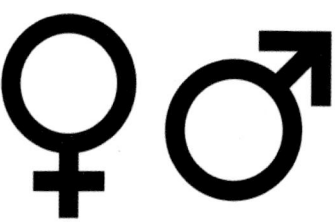

LOSING THINGS!

You lose your glasses and your keys,
and lose your tempers – sometimes true.
At least, you'll never lose our love,
and hope we make that clear to you!

Pets sometime lose our appetites,
and lose our toys? We do that too!
But one thing that we rarely lose
is huge respect and faith in you!

Yes, at times we lose our patience,
that's if a walk is getting rare,
but lose the will to tell you that –
if otherwise, you're more than fair.

To lose your friendship? Awful thought!
The *worst* thing any dog could do.
Most dogs would lose the will to live,
and lose that pretty quickly too.

We dogs may lose a lot of things,
but very rarely lose the plot,
and never lose our gratitude –
that's if we're clearly loved a lot.

A DOG'S VIEW OF CATS

Life's mostly fun for dogs like me.
It's much less fun to be a cat.
What? Never taken out for walks?
I don't think I could cope with that!

You sit on people's laps far more –
the only time I envy you.
It's rather nice to hear you purr.
I'd rather like to do that too!

Perhaps you need less company,
and like a walk upon your own.
That must be true, I'm sure it is,
as cats don't seem to moan and groan!

You don't like dogs – you make that clear.
We quickly learn to live with that.
And dogs are rarely fond of *you.*
We're not too keen on any cat!

But enemies? We rarely are.
And goodness me, why should we be,
if owners like both dogs and cats
and seem to love us equally?

A WORD WITH YOU!

How many words do we dogs know?
I'm not quite sure, but here's a list.
I know it isn't all that long.
There may be others that I've missed.

Out! Walkies! Up! Down! Catch! Off! Fetch!
Sit! Here! Drop! Yuk! Wait! Pooh! and Bed!
And yes, the words used in this verse.
But learning more? A thing we'd dread!

You children learn so many words.
But that's because you need to speak.
To count up all the ones you know
would take us *years*, not just a week!

We often wish that we could talk
and knew as many words as you.
But that will always be a dream,
and something that we'll never do.

Twenty words – our usual limit,
and most of us learn even less.
You think we dogs don't give a toss?
You're wrong! A source of huge distress!

And all the books upon your shelves
can often sadden dogs like me.
We'd love to read them, when you're out,
but can't – and so frustratingly!

TAILS

Why *don't* you humans have nice tails?
I guess you'd find it hard to dress.
Without a tail, we dogs would wail,
and live in terrible distress!

Our tails – the nicest part of us!
They help us to communicate,
and tell you we're enjoying life,
and live without one? *That* we'd hate!

What? Left without a tail to wag?
Gosh, what a drag our lives would be!
We need to have a tail to wag
to say we're living happily!

And if we aren't, our tails still help,
They make it clear we're cross with you.
And how? We just stop wagging them.
Then notice that? Most owners do!

Our waggy tails all make you smile,
and that's so nice for dogs to see,
and also clearly nice for you.
That's why we wag them frequently!

BARKING MAD

We bark with anger – and with joy,
and bark when someone's at the door,
and bark to greet you – and your friends.
There's always one more bark in store!

We bark when frightened or surprised,
and sometimes bark to wake you up,
and bark with fear from time to time,
and learn to bark when still a pup.

We bark each time the postman comes,
and bark at any sudden noise,
and bark with fury frequently –
that's when we've lost our favourite toys.

We bark with pleasure every time
you choose to take us on a walk,
and bark when spotting other dogs,
while often wishing we could talk.

We bark with joy, and every time
we see you picking up a lead,
and always bark at other dogs
who seem to be another breed.

We bark at dogs on TV shows,
especially ones who look like us,
and bark at other animals
which always makes you furious!

DEAF DOGS

These days, getting hard of hearing,
I wonder what my ears are for.
I often wish your kindly God
could think of giving me two more!

Owners – sometimes hard of hearing,
and yes, we should consider that,
but they just put on hearing aids –
which dogs can't do, nor any cat.

Hearing, when it's disappearing
is not the nicest thing to face,
and guessing there's no way to help
just makes my world a sadder place!

PATS AND STROKES

Please, please, more strokes, and on my head;
a thing we doggies all adore!
Just one a day is always nice,
but wish we got a whole lot more!

A gorgeous feeling on our fur.
In fact, each stroke is utter bliss.
And days without one? Disappointing –
they're ones we pets would rather miss!

I don't think humans even guess
they help to give us confidence.
You need to know (but rarely do)
the pleasure can be quite intense!

Uplifting, heartening, reassuring –
my goodness me, that's always true,
and as our owners ought to know,
they make us twice as fond of you!

SOMETHING THAT REALLY DOGS ME

With every single year that passes
I get more jealous of your glasses.
I can't see as I used to do,
or run as fast – that's also true.

Not quite knowing where I'm going
can be an awful misery.
Why are dogs not given glasses?
To me, that's such a mystery!

And why do you have hearing aids
but never put them on a pet?
That's something else I'd like to know.
Thank goodness I don't need them yet!

CATS AND DOGS

You say it's raining 'cats and dogs' –
that's if it's raining heavily.
But where are all the cats and dogs?
They're something that we never see.

In fact, we're very glad we don't.
What? Creatures falling from the sky?
That's not a thing we'd like to watch –
we'd hate to see them fall and die!

And goodness me, who's throwing them?
We can't believe it might be God.
And if it is, then what a shock!
All cats and dogs would find that odd.

I think it may be just a phrase –
that's if the rain is pelting down,
but still, they're horrid words for pets,
and ones that make our spirits drown!

SORRY FOR MYSELF

My master had to go to France,
and now my mistress is in bed –
and not because she wants to sleep.
She fell downstairs, and hit her head.

I shouldn't grumble, left alone,
not if her head is agony.
And if he's stuck in France for days,
at least, your neighbour's feeding me.

He's feeding my nice mistress too –
of course, a huge relief for me.
Without such help, what would I do?
I'd fade away – and so would she!

Dogs, perhaps, can be more selfish
than any of our owners are.
And grumble if they're not around?
Perhaps that's going much too far!

Are dogs self-centred? Possibly.
And should we think more outwardly?
Perhaps a thing we ought to learn
when owners need our sympathy.

YOUNG DOGS

Young dogs aren't fools; we learn the rules,
and things that you expect from us.
But that can take us several months,
which makes our owners furious!

We know we shouldn't bark at you -
except with joy. Mad thing to do!
But other rules can baffle me,
so please explain them – quickly, too!

All human children have to learn,
exactly as all puppies do.
But goodness me, we sometimes wish
we'd learn the rules as fast as you!

ONE THING WE KNOW

We know we shouldn't bark at you
(except with joy to see you back –
that's if you've been away all day).
Then, patience *is* a thing we lack!

But surely, that's forgivable.
No dogs much like it, left alone.
Like you, we all need company.
and hate it, left upon our own!

We wander round, but miserably,
and can't be bothered with our toys,
and when we hear you coming back,
that fast becomes our favourite noise!

The sound of keys, and in the lock?
What *heaven* for all pets like me!
Of course, we race up to the door
with tails all wagging frantically!

WHAT HUMANS LOVE

My mistress loves her friends around.
Her daughter clearly loves her doll.
And what's a thing my master likes?
An evening glass of alcohol!

And what do dogs like? Walks, of course,
and bones that we can pick with you
(and not because we're getting cross).
I mean the sort of bones we chew!

And humans can be favourite things,
as dogs can be – and frequently.
Otherwise, you wouldn't buy us.
We'd soon become a rarity!

Good behaviour – that's our saviour.
That makes us favourites, in a trice.
Obedience makes commonsense –
for other pets, our best advice!

'PET HATE'

Gosh – what a crazy thing to say!
Does anybody hate a pet?
Loved we are, and never hated.
That's true of every pet I've met!

Adore us? Yes, you mostly do,
and make that pretty clear to us.
But if you didn't, what a life!
We pets would be quite furious!

But when I dwell upon that phrase,
I think we *do* have one 'pet hate'.
But what? I'm pretty sure you know.
It's when you come back home so late!

I'M CROSS

Why *have* you bought another dog?
These days I'm full of jealousy.
I'll never be as happy now.
An only dog I'd rather be.

He gets a lot more strokes that me,
and probably as he's a pup.
And when he barks, it makes me cross.
My owners never say 'Shut up!'

I'd love to nip him, but I can't.
A thing I wouldn't dare to do.
I guess I'll just get used to him,
but find it hard – forgiving you.

We only dogs aren't lonely dogs
That's if we have your company.
I'd rather be an only pet.
More time to make a fuss of me!

JEALOUSY

I'm jealous of the dog next door.
He gets a lot more walks than me.
I often hear him bark for joy –
it's hard to stave off jealousy.

I'd love to be a friend of his,
but would he like my company?
Not if he guessed my jealousy.
He'd tire of me, and instantly!

I'd love to go for walks with him.
But does he know that? Probably.
His owners must have guessed that's true
from how I moan so pitifully!

DOGGIE FRIENDS

'Muffin', 'Tinka', 'Topsy', 'Danny' –
they're quite the nicest dogs I know.
But do they like me just as much?
How awful if they all said "No!"

I ought to guess that from their tails –
that's if they wag when seeing me,
and which they do, I'm glad to say –
and even better – instantly!

We need best friends, as humans do –
and kindly ones who cheer us up.
I've always known that from my birth.
First thing we learn, when born a pup!

Wriggling tummies? Barks of welcome?
What lovely things to hear and see!
Our owners surely feel the same,
but show their pleasure differently!

At least, we've got our tails to wag –
that's if we're in nice company.
And notice if they sag or wag?
Friends spot that – and immediately!

A TRIM, PLEASE!

I wish that you would trim my fur.
These days, I'm getting far too hot.
In Winter, I enjoy my coat.
But in the Summer – not a lot!

What a shame I can't use scissors,
as humans do – quite easily.
It's so unfair you cut your hair
without a single thought for me!

Gosh, phew, I'm hot! And nice, that's not!
The sun is sometimes *not* a friend.
In fact, at times, an enemy
who drives us dogs around the bend!

Life can be grim, without a trim,
and when we're feeling boiling hot,
especially if we're fluffy pets
and fed up with the coats we've got!

Before you own a hairy one,
make sure you own sharp scissors too,
and trim our coats from time to time.
Is that too much to ask of you?

CRAP

These days, when walking in the park,
you have to scoop up doggy poo,
and bag it up, or face a fine,
which surely means less walks with you.

What? Take a plastic bag with you
and clear up what you call my 'crap'?
I know my owner won't do that.
He's simply not that sort of chap.

What faster way to spoil a walk?
I certainly can't think of one.
And nor could owners – that's for sure.
A certain way to spoil their fun.

Oh well, a lot less walks for me
and other dogs I used to see.
Who *were* the fools who made such rules,
and made our walks a misery?

Has no-one noticed when we poo
we do that well away from you
and very rarely on the path?
A thing we know we shouldn't do!

Or why not build a doggy loo –
a place where we can pee or poo,
and furthermore, in privacy,
as every dog prefers to do!

THE PAVEMENT

Puddles, puddles, everywhere –
but not a drop to drink.
And why? It might be doggie pee.
Best left alone, we think!

It's hard to tell, without a smell.
A risk we shouldn't take.
It's best to wait, until we're home;
not make a big mistake!

But what to do if parched by thirst
and need to drink – and fast?
Just turn around and hurry home,
until we're there – at last!

Yes, of course that baffles owners
when tugging at the lead.
They never guess when turning round,
a drink is what we need!

We always know what humans do
when desperate for a drink.
You hurry off to nearby pubs,
at least, that's what dogs think.

The very thought of drinking pee –
enough to make me sick!
Puddles – always risky things.
Not one is worth a lick!

GOLDEN OLDIES

We fear it's near – our time to go,
with no more dogs we'd want to know,
and things we don't much want to do –
like going on long walks with you.

We'd rather be in bed instead,
and dreaming of our younger years –
when racing and outpacing you,
and sometimes driving you to tears!

We'd love to show our gratitude,
but find that rather hard to do,
while hoping you don't find it rude
if only wagging tails for you.

When getting old, and good as gold,
we're happy just to live with you.
No-one else would want to own us,
as faithful owners always do!

OH DEAR!

'I don't think that he'll make old bones' –
I heard you say that yesterday.
I hope you weren't describing me,
and think I might soon pass away.

I think I'm ten, yes, ten years old,
but surely I'm too young to die.
How long do dogs live? I don't know.
I've never known, and wonder why.

Perhaps they're thinking of a friend.
All I can do is hope that's true.
My bones are fine; they seem to work,
and give me hell, they never do.

I don't have any aches and pains,
and never find a day a slog
as older humans often do.
Thank God I'm still a healthy dog!

Old bones I'd never want to make –
that's if they're things you want to chew.
My goodness, what a ghastly thought!
I dearly hope that isn't true!

I never need a walking frame
as ancient humans seem to do,
but still, they're rather fun to use -
to help us stand up straight like you!

LEGS

Gosh, why do humans have two legs?
I'm sure you'd like another two.
What? Walking upright all the time?
I'm sure that's sometimes hard for you.

Of course, you sit down now and then,
and when you're old, that's often true.
Another pair of legs might help,
but grow two more? You never do!

For dogs, our legs are miracles.
We're always pleased we're born with four.
They help us balance brilliantly,
and stop us falling on the floor!

What's more, four legs can help us run,
and sometimes at amazing speed.
It's strange you never want two more.
Two legs, it seems, are all you need!

But then, you always have two arms,
so never need four legs like me.
Yes, the more I think about it,
it helps to solve the mystery!

CRUFTS

Now children, have you heard of Crufts?
You haven't? Then it's time to know
it's where we dogs can win a prize
if we're the best ones in the show.

We have to be obedient
and show off things that we can do.
And if we do that brilliantly,
we might bring home a prize for you!

A shiny cup – most likely one
to put up somewhere on your shelves,
and where we dogs can gaze at it
and then congratulate ourselves!

Dog shows – these days, getting rarer –
a fact that doesn't bother me.
A silver cup to cheer me up
is not a thing I need to see!

I think I'm quite a handsome dog.
I guess that from the strokes I get.
But test that out, and in a show?
I'd be a most unhappy pet!

I don't think any dogs I've met
are prone to what's called 'vanity'.
As long as owners like our looks,
we'll live with them quite happily!

MY MASTER

My master's gone to 'hospital'.
But what's that? Gosh, I wish I knew.
A place to go to, if you're ill?
I dearly hope that isn't true.

He used to take me out for walks.
My mistress used to do that too.
But now I'm mostly stuck at home,
because she goes to visit you.

How many years do people live?
Much longer, I thought, than dogs do.
But now it seems I may be wrong.
I'm worried stiff about you two.

But only think about myself?
That's something I should never do.
I guessed that many months ago.
But goodness, I'm afraid for you!

I'd place a bet a loving pet
would speed up your recovery.
But doctors wouldn't think of that,
with things that take priority.

DREAMS

All dogs have dreams, as humans do,
but don't have the same ones as you.
We mostly dream we're off the lead.
A favourite dream? Of course, that's true!

Exploring, roaming round alone –
that's always our most common one.
In fact, it's such a blissful dream
that waking up is not much fun!

Once again, we're in the kitchen
and waking in the same old bed,
while wishing we could use the key
and free to roam outside instead!

Gosh, what a wheeze to steal your keys!
Of course, a dream that won't come true.
Not least because you hang them up
in places we can't reach like you.

A GRANNY

A Granny? What on earth is that?
That's something pets would love to know.
They seem to be such pleasant friends,
and ones you've known since years ago.

They're always older than you are,
and often a lot wiser too.
I love it when they come and stay.
They stroke us more than owners do!

Do dogs have Grannies? I don't know.
If so, they're ones we've never met.
It can be terribly frustrating
to be a dog or other pet!

Pets so rarely know our parents,
and let alone, grandparents too.
Not many owners sympathize –
a thing they always ought to do!

Just thinking of our families
can so upset a dog or cat.
That's if we never get to meet.
My goodness me, how sad is that?

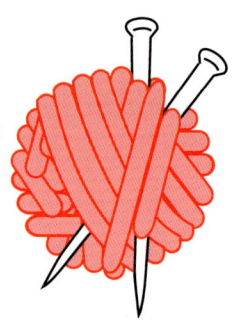

JOBS

My lovely owners both have jobs
that help them live more comfortably.
But I think the best job they do
is simply looking after me!

I also have a job to do,
and what's more, an important one.
But what? You humans ought to know.
It's making all your lives more fun!

I like to think that's what I do,
a thought that always comforts me.
And if I didn't? Gosh, how sad –
I'd live in utter misery!

You humans can be quite hard work,
though not a thing you realize.
Perhaps a thankyou now and then?
Now, that would be a nice surprise!

A DOGGIE DREAM

Last night I dreamed that I was human,
and had two legs like humans do.
And goodness, what a gorgeous dream!
What fun it was to stand like you!

Walking on 'all fours' is boring,
though other dogs might not agree.
That's if they are bigger, taller –
and not a little dog like me!

What? Scuttling round upon the floor?
That's not a thing I like to do.
I'd love to learn to stand up straight –
and play guitars like humans do!

However difficult it seems,
please try and understand my dreams.
Is that too much to ask of you?
I dearly hope that isn't true!

SHEEP DOGS

Our job is looking after sheep
and making sure they never stray.
That's if they try to wander off.
That keeps us busy every day.

We round them up – and speedily,
that's if they try to hide away –
or ever try to smash a fence,
fed up with where they're forced to stay.

We'd hate a life without a job.
How very dull each day would be!
What? Sit around in someone's house
with no responsibility?

We'd find it hell, stuck in a town,
and walking round it on a lead.
Life's far more fun for dogs with jobs.
That's why we're such a happy breed!

RESPECT

Of course, we dogs look up to you.
There's little else that we can do.
And why? That's not a mystery.
We never grow as tall as you!

Respect is something you expect.
But when we all look up to you,
it might be due to one thing – height,
and not our admiration too.

You may think you're superior,
as many of our owners do.
But when you all look down on us,
it's best not to assume that's true!

A MYSTERY

You own a boxer dog like me?
I'm sure he wags his tail for you.
But ever punch you with a paw?
The *last* thing that he'd ever do!

I've seen men boxing on TV
and knocking their opponents out.
It's not a sport I want to see,
or even want to think about!

What? Punching people in the face?
That's such a nasty thing to do.
It's something that a boxer dog
would *never* do to them – or you!

No, box we don't, and punch we won't,
which should be a relief for you.
All boxers are such friendly things
and fond of human beings, too!

You own a boxer dog like me?
I'm sure he wags his tail for you,
and does that pretty frequently,
as dogs like me all love to do!

WHY?

Why *do* you humans like us dogs?
It's not as if we talk to you,
or ever help you round the house.
What's more, we're quite expensive too!

You live with creatures like yourself.
But why live with a dog as well?
What makes us dogs so popular?
For us, it's pretty hard to tell.

Perhaps you like our company
because we think so differently,
and unlike you, have tails to wag
to say we're living happily.

Of course, we think of things like that,
although you never think we do.
In many ways, we're just like you.
If only all our owners knew!

Or maybe it's the exercise
you might not get without a pet.
A walk alone can't be much fun.
And glad of that? Oh yes, you bet!

CHRISTMAS

Christmas? Not the greatest time.
With luck, we'll get a choc or two,
but never at all other times.
I don't know any dogs who do.!

But do we get nice things instead?
Perhaps some scraps of turkey meat –
leftovers scraped from every plate.
But nothing tasting nice and sweet!

And ever get a Christmas gift?
Few owners ever give us one.
You clearly think dogs never mind
which doesn't make the day much fun.

It's nice to see your Christmas tree –
That helps to cheer us up a bit,
But not that much, and not enough.
A fun day? Quite the opposite!

A happy Christmas? Not for dogs.
In fact, a day we rather dread.
Small wonder that we slink away
and mostly spend the time in bed!

SPOTS

I'm a dog called a dalmation,
best known for all my lovely spots.
How many? Goodness, I don't know!
I only know that I've got lots!

You'll never ever count my spots,
no, because I'm far too spotty.
And if you tried to count them up,
that would drive you children potty!

All dalmations, such sensations!
What? Live without a single spot?
A load of other creatures do,
and jealous of them? No, we're not!

HAPPINESS

No dogs are happy *all* the time.
We get our 'down days' – just like you.
But humans never notice that.
You can't believe that might be true.

You wonder why we've gone to bed
and don't want human company.
but just assume we may be tired,
not facing bouts of misery.

The very fact we get depressed
might be a big surprise for you.
We rather hope you read this book
to learn we get our 'down days' too.

It doesn't mean we're cross or bored
or somehow feeling ill that day.
It's best to leave us in our beds,
until the blues just fade away!

DROOLING

We know it isn't cool to drool.
That's something we must never do.
So don't bring out the biscuit tin!
Is that too much to ask of you?

Biscuits? Lovely! Always scrummy!
Or course we drool – and instantly.
And if you hate us doing that,
don't put a tin in front of me!

Christmas? Lovely! What a time!
It's when we get a few from you,
but rarely at all other times.
I don't know any dogs who do!

FULL OF BEANS

You tell your friends I'm full of beans,
but full of them, I'm firmly not.
I've never, ever, eaten them,
though you two do, and quite a lot!

A dish of beans, gosh what a treat!
But something that I never eat.
Why lie to friends about my food,
when all I ever eat is meat?

I often see you eat baked beans,
but never put them in my bowl.
I'd love my tummy full of beans.
I know I'd be a happy soul!

GIGGLING

Dogs like me would love to giggle.
All we ever do is wriggle –
that's if we're finding something fun.
No dogs can giggle – no, not one!

Thank goodness we've got tails to wag.
If not, our lives would be a drag.
What? No way to say we're happy?
Goodness, that would make us snappy!

P.S.
Next time that you get the giggles,
please spare a thought for dogs like me.
Of *course* we love to hear you laugh,
but can't help pangs of jealousy!

IN PRAISE OF POVERTY

Humans who are short of money
make better owners in my view.
They eat out less, and travel less.
Good news for dogs like me and you.

They don't have second homes abroad,
and where they stay for weeks, or more;
and don't go shopping all the time.
Much nicer owners, that's for sure.

They can't afford another pet,
so lavish far more time on us.
Poorer owners - always better.
The plus points are quite numerous.

They can't afford a boarding school,
so children stay at home with us.
We're never short of company.
And that's the most important plus!

GOODBYE FOR NOW!

'All good things come to an end!
Something that you humans say.
What's more, we agree with you.
Time to put our pens away!

Will we write another book?
Maybe. That depends on you.
If you liked this book, we might.
Wait and see – best thing to do!

Other books by Liz Cowley

Outside in My
Dressing Gown

and other poems for garden lovers
by Liz Cowley

What am I
Doing Here?
more poems by
Liz Cowley

'Quick wit and
sharp observations'

illustrations by Terrance.

DONOUGH O'BRIEN & LIZ COWLEY

"The authors delve into little known, but really significant,
corners of history that highlight human frailty and unpredictability."
Christopher Joll
Author and Historian

DREAMS
DELUSIONS&
DISASTERS
THE BOOK OF MISFORTUNES

From sex to money,
from politics to sport,
fateful decisions that
went badly wrong